descendant

romeo romero

oceanmouth publishing

mxromeoromero@gmail.com

Cover Image © 2018 by Nina Yagual

Logo Image © 2018 by Elaine Mehary

First Printing, 2018

ISBN 978-1-7323761-0-6

http://mxromeoromero.com
oceanmouth publishing

Gratitude//Acknowledgements

Thank you to my ancestors who have always held me. Thank you to my sibling, Amy, for carrying our lineage with me and for teaching me to be the person I need to be (and for being my #1 editor). Thank you to my mother and father for the most ferocious and consistent love. Thank you to my chosen family—Gracynn Gray, Kyan, Emmett, Marisol—for belonging with me in this world. Thank you to my love, Sylas, for choosing to heal with me every day. Thank you to my mentors over all of the years—Vero, Safire, Layla, Kristen, Ling, Tara, Antonio—for your grounded wisdom, for showing me how to listen to the knowledge all around us, and for always centering joy and well-being in how we move. Thank you to the Pa'lante students who teach me every day what it means dream and love together.

This project would not be possible without the commitment and support of so many people. I am honored and deeply moved by all of the energy and collaboration that went into the birth of this book.

Amy Sigle, editor
Shady Kimzey, publicist
Nina Yagual, cover artist
Elaine Mehary, logo artist
Camila Lourdes, launch party extraordinaire
Marisol Fernandez y Mora, proof-reader
Abner Aldarondo, proof-reader

Topography//Contents

What to Expect from this Book//Foreword

Hi! My name is Romeo. Thank you for holding my heart in your hands today.

You might be wondering a little bit about who I am and where this book came from. I wonder that too, sometimes.

Here's the barest bones:

I'm a descendant of the Boricua and Jewish diasporas.

My mother's people come from a small island off the coast of Puerto Rico called Vieques. My father's people most recently come from Russia, several generations ago.

My parents were both raised in New York City in the 60s and 70s. I was born in New York in the 90s and moved to Washington State as a teenager. (I've since embraced myself as a tender west-coaster.)

I began writing because it's the only way I knew how to make sense of myself as a descendant of peoples I may never know. I use writing to dive deep into grief, my body, colonization/genocide/intergenerational trauma, gender, magic, and love. I use writing to reclaim myself from a world that constantly tries to re-write who I am.

In this book, you will find a collection of poems, a sprinkling of prose, and spells for our peoples. The collection spans 10 years (roughly 2008-2018). As you might expect, I no longer agree with everything written in this book (and don't anticipate that you will, either). But, every piece offered me deep healing at the time it was written, and thus I have chosen to share them with you. If any part of *descendant* resonates with you, I encourage you to reach out and let me know. (Connection is the purpose of art, after all.) My email is mxromeoromero@gmail.com.

Spell #1: On Beginnings

I invite my ancestors and the universe that have always held me to join me in making space for change and in remaining open to the possibilities that lie ahead.

In this time of new beginnings, I am beginning to believe that I deeply belong in the places I find myself. I am beginning to believe that with so much to do, we can all do some things that matter. I am beginning to believe that healing is not only possible, but inevitable.

Let's Start Simple.
Repeat After Me:
Know Your Enemy
Revolutionize
Reinvent
& Love Every Shiver-Inducing Yes.

Broken Poetry

Once, a nationally award-winning poet told me
that self-indulgent poetry
(poetry about race, madness, revolution)
belongs in diaries or in therapy.

Fuck her.

This is not a poem for her.
This is a poem for people like me
who need a place
to scream.
I don't water down my throat for anybody.

We have not been born poets.
We are born with bones like eggshells.
We are born with skin like satin.
The first poem we wrote gave us our backbone
written up from the first moment that made us feel
like we had more worth than the earth we stood on.
Or less than it.

This poetry was built for intimacy.
Don't let the stage fool you.
This poetry is just a bunch of secrets.

Once, the dentist told me
that the cure for my aching head
was locked inside my jaw.
She said it looked like I'd been chewing on sand
biting through walls of concrete.

I fit city streets in my cheeks
gentrification between my teeth
the united states military could not bust through the muscle
by emptying their guns
into my gums.
My mouth is full of violence.

I think my mother gave me more
than brown eyes
and a fear of cockroaches.

She gave me a fear of the government
(but hoped I'd never speak of it).

I used to talk loud on the playground
but they beat the voicebox right out of me
so I'd never tell you who did it.

Now here's a secret—
bullies,
boyfriends,
and countries
use all the same tactics
to keep their victims quiet.

This poetry is not art.

There is no sense striving to make something beautiful
out of the rupture of body from spirit.
So place the shame between your teeth
and bite down on the kyriarchy's wrists.
Tell them how it feels to be wishful.

Spit to flesh
Spit truth to flesh
Don't spit for nothing.

Our ancestors did not learn to master their tongues
so that we could talk small.
Language was born to bear witness
to all that had been left unnamed before.

So, name yourself.
Name what makes you hurt.
If this is the only medication you can afford
then write yourself the prescription.
There is a remedy
waiting in your mouth.

Go ahead.
Write your broken poetry.
Write the words you were afraid
even the paper could not hold.

You are wisdom unfolding.
You are a roundhouse kick to the solar plexus.
You are consciousness brewing.

Your body is not art.
You are not up for debate.
There is no right way to come
face-to-face with pain.

So, if you mean every word that you say
instead of calling it a poem
I want to call it

necessary.

Captive

Another world can't come unless we're willing to let this one go.
Still, I am off the wrong edge of the earth.
I am off the edge,
yet I tighten my grip.

Who were you to tell me I could find answers in the oldest bone?
I am like the ancestors' trees.
I am slowly dying from the toxic air that I breathe.
I am waiting for parental guidance,
for godly advice.
I am soiling,
becoming some kind of mud.

Can you hear the way the water runs?
Slowly, like there's no chase.
Slowly, like there's nowhere left to go.
I wonder what that feels like.
I wonder what it feels like to slow.

There are blisters in my roots;
I grip the ground and am mercilessly torn up.
It hurts to remember those times.
It hurts to remember the way the earth could let me go so easy.
Sometimes I want to learn this skill.
Other times I want to never repeat the mistake.

I gave up expression about the same time I gave up suicide.
I'd drink to that.
I'd drink to being present,
to feeling joy in my body before it lets me go, too.
Relentless suffering sits in my bones and I know that's a scorpio thing to say,
but I can't stop saying it.

I know hurting must be seasonal.
Like depression.
Like affect.
I wonder how anyone could settle into despair like this.
How anyone could settle for winter.
How anyone could settle upon someone else's land.
Please.

Rip me up before I learn this violence.
Rip me up before I find a home that way.
I promise you,
I can nurse myself back whole.

My ancestors told me once that water only feels like ice when you're not
used to it.
Warmth comes in time,
comes from letting the waves lick at your wounds.
Let the ocean get to know you.
Fill me up starting with the deepest cut.
I'd let the riptide take me.
I'd let the currents carry me away.
Caress this body for the first time.

You could save me once.
You could save me many times,
but save it for a rainy day.
You can hold me tender 'til then.
You can hold me hostile, too.
It may not make a difference.
Every claw has a paw, every talon a feather.
I know that there must be something soft underneath this armor.
I know there must be something hard underneath the spineless.
I'm not sorry for all the ways I don't make sense.
I'm not sorry for seeing things at night.
I'm not sorry you see hope where I see another dead end.
We are standing on opposite sides of the fence.
I've got magic pulling me somewhere.
I've got chains around my wrists.
Can you feel the weight of that?

Captured can't let go.
I whimper softly in the cage you call home.
Your cells are made of iron,
oxygen keeps binding me to ore.
There's a ghost, pulling in to harbor.
There's an ocean in my chest.
Anchor clacks against rib.
Can you feel the weight of it?

descendant

Captive,
take the chains off.
Captor,
let this one go.

fear, let go

I'm no longer afraid
of believing in people
or believing in their intuition.
I'm not afraid of asking a hard question
or asking the wrong question.
I'm not afraid of directing my questions
to both science
and the ocean.
And to you,
I'd ask you:
hey, haven't we met before?
and, would you ever believe that time could be cyclical
because if ghosts are dead,
how'd you learn to haunt me like that?

I'm still afraid of ghosts.

But, I'm no longer afraid of responding to my name
or responding to those who may never say it.
I'm not afraid of arguing with a reason
or anger without a reason.
I'm not afraid of being unreasonable
because whoever made the decision
that logic takes more strength than emotion
never felt the irrefutable pull
of two minds in love.
Or instead, they chose to ignore
the anchoring of lonely
weighing in their veins
and to peel desire from tissue
as if it were born from disease
until all of their wanting
would have turned into haunting
of the person whose love they can't bear to concede.

And, I'm still afraid of blood.

But, I'm no longer afraid of seeing scars
or people seeing my scars.
I'm not afraid of being a scar

in the memories of those I've failed to heal
because I've told you over and over again
that people cannot be burdens.

And, if you scream at me for burning down your walls
and not being the one to build them back up,
I will remind you that you are not a building
and you are not under construction
and metaphors work well in poetry
but not in explanations
for why people do the things they do
and feel like it's time to leave
and forget how to tell you
why they ever stayed at all.

And, I'm still afraid to go.

Though, that may be why I don't want to go backwards
if you'd ever believe that time could be cyclical
then, maybe, I'd see you tomorrow.

My Breath is in My Hands

My breath is in my hands
and I am encaged,
enraged, engaged with the fingers
slowly paging through the history
that's been embedded in the base of my spine—

They drive
their pen into my neck
carving lines through all that I
forget, this mess of
crossing out the poems in my
mind, I grind my teeth
to keep from biting off their wrists
and I send this anger to my palms—
my breath
is in my hands.

I am fractured. This body tells a broken story.
You've come for the wrong one, I say.
If I could crawl deep into the
hollows of my bones,
and find that my mother's mother's mother
still passes through me with every exhale,
I'd spend every day wandering those tunnels
and calling her name.
I'd search the walls for all the messages
she scrawled in the undersides of my skin…
but, I wasn't taught to read the language that she spoke in.

My bones erode and I've grown foreign.
I cannot tell you the truth
that's been whispered into my blood.
They can excavate my body
take away my story
hold me like an artifact—
I may endure the burns
that have passed into my birth
but I ache for every word
I never learned, so I'm sure
I'll never give them what they're looking for.

Let me take all this shame
into my palms—
my breath
is in my hands.

I breathe
every chance I get
and I reach to mi familia
who has been colonized,
sterilized, excised—
who has watched every child
brought to America
be whitened,
told we can rise to the top
if we just give up
being brown.

But I know we won't exchange our blood so easy.
My mother and my sister
still cry with each other.
And I am encaged,
enraged, engaged with the flames
that tried to choke the fight right out of me.
I awoke and the smoke
may have ruined my lungs, but I wrote
the poems that were hidden in my thumbs.
There's a lot
of breath
left in these hands—
enough
to hold my pen.

Moon Prayer

Does she know
that there are still a few of us left
who speak of her
as measurement?

For many moons ago,
she was the only
measurement.

For a long time, I wondered
how it might feel to be calculated
as accurately as the Moon.
To be dutiful, devoted.
So that those who count on me
won't lose track.

Mama

Mama,
my hair is coarser than my father's
but not as coarse as yours
so I am reminded that your blood
is coursing through my veins
and that the course we're on
isn't always easy.

Mama,
you went to school to be a teacher
but teaching kids doesn't pay enough to raise your kids
so you stayed home
and taught me everything you could.

Mama,
I never could figure out how to roll my Rs,
so I practiced my lullabies all wrong
and instead of turning Rs into Zs
Americanized tears rolled down my cheeks
and I never once learned to sing myself to sleep.

Mama,
I know I threw a lot of temper tantrums
but maybe I just never found a way to breathe
and as I got older
I started eating my temper like it was part of my diet
until my diet consisted of nothing but air and a bottle of anger.

Mama,
you told me once that growing older
isn't an exact science
and the older I get the surer I get
that nothing ever is.
While they may waste time debating
the chemistry of contagion
we know deep down
they're just contemplating the chemistry of their own hearts.

Mama,
America taught me to be easy
and I think they tried to teach you the same
but instead of drinking bottles of anger
wondering why we can't fix all of the harm,
will you teach me how to sing?
I know the course we're on
isn't always easy
but will you come with me
so we can both just learn how to breathe.

November 9th, 2016

We are in the thick of collective trauma right now. Those of us who are people of color, immigrants, queer, trans, disabled, rape survivors, people at the margins. White supremacy is yelling from the top of its lungs now. We can't escape how it feels about us.

Many of us are born out of violent histories. Fear of white supremacy has been written into our blood. Our reactions today are not based on irrationality. They are based on memory. Ancestral trauma is the way that we remember what resistance feels like. How bad it hurts to fight.

I am in pain because the world is in pain. I am in pain because we've been here before. I am in pain because actually, we have never been given a fucking break.

I consider myself a community-care-taker. I consider myself a trauma & healing worker. From a spiritual standpoint, I consider my life and my energy to be bound up with yours.

As the election results came in, my response was, I don't know what to do. I don't know what we can do now.

I have a chosen family back on the West Coast...queer, trans, disabled, folks of color. I'm not used to having nothing to say to offer comfort. I'm not used to being at a loss for words. But today, when my family announced how unsafe they feel, how violated they feel, how terrified they feel. I could not console, I could only bear witness.

I ask myself: what does healing look like now. For some people, we grieve by taking action. For others, we hold each other close and remind ourselves we are not alone. We ask each other not to die, not to give up. For others, we remember to eat. We remember to breathe. We stay off Facebook. We continue to exist.

For me, healing looks like committing to never again saying, I don't know what to do.

We know what to do.

Oppression keeps us separate. The biggest fuck you that we can ever give to white supremacy is to reach out for each other and say: I've got you. And I need you.

We know what to do because our bodies remember what to do. Our bodies remember because here we all are. Right now, we hold the answers.

We are powerful forces, we are energy erupting, we are connected. We remember another world is still possible, together, and we remember how to fight for it.

White Supremacy Poem #1: On being qtpoc and working in a university// this is how racial capitalism works

My supervisor has a rainbow flag sticker on her door.
It says "hate free zone."
She calls me an amazing woman
every time she introduces me to someone new.
And I am too afraid to correct her
on my pronouns
on my gender
on me.
Because
she is another white woman
working with brown kids.

And I am a brown kid
who now works for her.

White Supremacy Poem #2: Why solidarity with white women is so difficult

When someone says to me:
"I know the pain you face as a person of color,
because I am a woman."
I know they would never see me
also,
as a woman.

White Supremacy Poem #3: When a white person calls me angry

I'm not angry,
I lie.

Because if I don't,
they walk away
believing they were right.

And if they are right about the anger
then they'll think that they are right
about everything.

White Supremacy Poem #4: The Order of Things

If you say anything about "white people,"
the way they flock to defend their own
is proof enough
that they have a stake
in maintaining
the order of things.

White Supremacy Poem #5: After

After you scold me for my pain
I write poems about it.
Tell me:
what good
have you done
with your whiteness.

Spell #2: On Nourishing the Body

I invite my ancestors and the universe that have always held me to bring me strength and clarity in this moment, and to support me in embodying the following truths.

1. My body exists exactly as it is meant to, at the exact size it is meant to be.
2. White supremacy demands us to engage in acts of comparison and inadequacy and preoccupation. I will resist the urge to feed white supremacy with these actions.
3. My body need not look like other bodies. Being brown and big and soft is beautiful. It is exactly how I want to be.
4. My body is wise, it knows better than my head what it needs, so I must listen to it. It is unique—it needs differently than all other bodies. I will listen to my hunger and my desire in order to nourish my body with everything it wants. I will resist the guilt that comes with giving myself what I need in a world that has tried to keep me starving.
5. My body has no binary gender. I feel out of place here because I have chosen to honor the truth of my body and of my gender. This is noble—this is my bravest choice. Fitting into this society may be seductive, but it is deadly, and I will not kill any part of myself to feel like I belong in a culture that has been complicit in such violence.
6. As a queer person of color, feeling my difference and my bigness is powerful; it is a sign that I am no longer hiding my physical and spiritual beings from myself; these beings are integral parts of the universe, and they are all mine.
7. I exist for a great purpose; to heal and to be healed; I will not get confused about that; I will focus my energy on this path.

I am different. I am wise. I am vast. I am mine. I am purpose embodied. I am my body. I am my ancestors' body. I am a very, very sacred thing.

Diasphoria

I both am
and am not
a woman.

That's how it is for those of us
with colonized wombs.
That's how it is for those of us
with wounds on the inside of our bellies
where genocide shakes hands with the patriarchy.

That's how it is for those of us
who've lost the words to name ourselves
to lay claim to the valleys in our bones.

> Diaspora is very much a gender thing.
> It is very much a body thing.
>
> Being trans is kind of like being forgotten.
> Migration is kind of like being force-fed forget.
>
> My body aches to be somewhere it is not.
> My body aches to be something it is not.
>
> Some days it feels like I will never have a homeland,
> like my body will never be a homeland.
>
> It hurts so much to forget.
> So much more to remember.
>
> I may never know who I've been.
> I may never become who I am.

We will name ourselves in response
to the world we've been put in.
Our names are leftover desires
for a world we can never have back.
They are our war cries, our loyalty, our refusal.
This is how I say no to being taken.

descendant

I am not just one thing.
I am not just one time.
I am many things.
I am all the time.

Ugly Things

I shower every day.
Sometimes twice.
My best friend used to buy foundation
lighter than her skin tone
because she wanted to be white enough to marry someday.

I know that feeling.

White hot anger escapes the dying breath of an immigrant father
when the realization finally comes:
he couldn't make it better for anyone.

There are still cobwebs in my throat
from the three years I spent forgetting how to cry.
Sometimes daughters can't look their mothers in the eye
when they want to be held.
Instead they yell
pick fights from the silver in their cavities
the bleeding in their gums
they lunge
straight for the aorta
they win.

You breathe in dust every time you open up her baby book.
She isn't coming back to us.
We were baptized under east coast foliage.
The water fell from gorges that sometimes struggled to make ends meet.
I was taught that scarcity is a blessing.
So, I've never asked for more than I've been given,
the hunger
drives the weakest to believe that exchanging pleasantries
is a sign of affection.
I became affectionate with everyone.

I never sent thank you cards.
I never thanked my ancestors for giving me good genes,
a gentle tongue,
or angrier teeth.

I lie with the best of them,
pull rank like it'll get me somewhere.
The rut only gets deeper from here.

We're not going to paris.
We're not going to the moon.
We faked it through high school,
faked falling in love.
Because having a sweetheart who writes you love notes in pencil
is better than getting no love notes at all.

I lit up when he looked at me.
I was light enough to marry someday.
I was indulging on the scarcity he gave me,
getting full on the idea
that I could really be something.

I lost my first set of marbles to him.
He won them fair and square right along with my dignity.
Or, I gave that one willingly.

It felt like catching skin
underneath the bike chain.
Gears don't stop turning if you scream.
I didn't scream.

The blood would harden in a day,
if you don't pick at the scabs.
I picked at the scabs.
I found out the secret about falling in love with placeholders.

These are the ugly things. We tie them to stones and give them to the
bay. We drown them. Bury them with the ashes of our least significant
lovers. Murder them with the same forks we use to eat our breakfast.
We've built them into our alibies. Tucked them neatly into our spines.
We've sewn them into the seams of our sobering minds. We'll
remember you come morning. We'll remember you come migraines and
seizures—the brain damage will reveal you. We'll remember you come
soldiers returning to their beds. We'll remember the war you left. And
when we do, I don't want to scour my body for any bullets I may have
missed. I'll wash the panic down with Adderall. I'll be up all night for
this. Waiting for you to call me like you did when we were kids. But
tonight,

I refuse
to thank you
for the bruises.

Spiders

watch the spider sew in the window
a web//trap//home
wonder if it ever tires of this one purpose
wonder if it ever wants to crawl into a corner to wither

lay upon your lover
and repeat the words over and over:
"I'm just so fucking sad"
make a promise together not to die
until you figure out a better way to live
link pinkies, kiss thumbs
don't die today
don't die making promises you know you can't keep

get a tattoo to say goodbye
because everything is temporary
even this body
write a poem about suicide
and hold yourself in all the places
no one else ever could

say goodbye to the ringing in your ears
say goodbye to the aching in your ovaries
say goodbye to the nightmares etched into your thumbprints
lust for visions
lust for the sweet smell of dementia
lust for atmosphere lodged in your esophagus
burst into your body
scream vulgar on the floor
let your eyes stay open
you don't need them any more than you need love

beg to be like a spider
wear your skin like you wear your armor
look your dinner in the eye
and seduce it
be too scary to crush between wall and shoe

know that you are utterly alone here
know that you are stunningly alone

when they find you in the corner
tell them about spiders
tell them about losing blood
write a poem about suicide
and tell them you made a promise not to die

Reflections on Suicide (2016)

5 years ago today, I was discharged from the hospital after surviving a suicide attempt. I almost didn't make it to my 18th birthday. I was one of the many queer teenagers in this world who tried to die.

I think often about those who didn't survive. And I think often about those who continue to experience the trauma of forced hospitalization and waking up to another day of being alive even though they don't want to. My heart will always ache, will always be entwined with those we grieve for and those who (like me) continue to survive this unique kind of trauma.

I have spent the past 5 years being a scorpio and transforming my pain into something beautiful. I know that my pain isn't my fault, that none of this was my fault. I have become a person that I want to be; I love myself, care for myself, and am committed to my well-being. I have experienced deep and profound love that I know many people spend their whole lives wishing for. Connection/intimacy/Magic/spirituality/my multiple incredible and inspiring families/my commitment to this world, is what keeps me going.

And yet, I still struggle with suicidality often. I still struggle with believing I can make it another day. Sometimes the pain from trauma and oppression,,, the queer diaspora feelings of *not belonging here*,,, are overwhelming.

Recovery is 100% a myth. There is no way for me to recover a body or a spirit that existed before my trauma, before my suicide attempt, before my hospitalization, before the medical abuse and neglect. There is nothing left to recover, I can only (re)create.

I'm not writing this because I need any "congrats for surviving" sentiments. I'm writing this because…I didn't think I'd ever be 22. I didn't think I'd ever grow up. I didn't think there was a place for me in this world. And I'm trying to embrace the wrong-ness of that. I'm still trying to create a different way of knowing and of being. One that doesn't involve me constantly dancing with death. 5 years is a long time to survive. 5 years, for me, has felt like a lifetime. And the weird thing is, that I *can* imagine myself existing in 5 more years. Some might call that an achievement, but in some ways maybe I'm just lucky.

Even more importantly, I think I'm writing this because there is still so much silence, and so much invulnerability, and so much fear about talking about suicide. Being a suicide survivor has been an important part of my identity, and yet it is one I very rarely talk about publicly. Because those who have not had this experience continue to stigmatize, get uncomfortable, offer pity, or sometimes even act out in violence towards us.

After I got discharged 5 years ago, I immediately went back to college. I somehow finished the quarter with a 4.0. I pretended that this never happened. I put arbitrary measures of success over my own healing. And in so many ways I continue to do this—I continue to do what is expected of me while living my life as if *this never happened to me*.

Only it did happen. And I am 100% the person I am today because it happened. And I don't want to keep myself a secret anymore. I don't want my history to be unknown by people who *think* they know me. I don't want to lie about the person that I *still* am.

I am letting go of the shame associated with my history. I am not a failure for attempting suicide. I am not a failure because my suicide attempt was *only* an attempt. I am not a failure for still hurting, 5 years later…for not recovering, for still fighting.

I'm not looking to rewrite myself as a success story. I just want to acknowledge that my life, as I continue to live it (even as I often do not *want* to live it) is ok. Is still valid. Is still something worth talking about.

All that being said,,, here's to my younger self, who didn't know what I know now, but who felt everything so deeply that it almost killed her.

& I think that's pretty cool.

Ghosts in my Body

I've been talking to the ghosts in my walls again.
I wait for a day that they, too, will touch me heavy-handed
like oil rigs tearing at the heart of this earth
as she silently screams in sacrifice.

I've tried to exorcize her sound from my dreams,
to write ballads to the people I used to be,
to imagine revolution,
and feel close to her.
Like god.

But transgression holds me hostage.
My body\\ is home to too many ghosts,
and you are asking to be another.
I can feel my seams bursting just to hold you,
to give you shelter, to give you more than a body should give.

In this world,
I cannot belong solely to myself.
Too many have killed off their sweetest echo
and left it between my ribs to rot.
My mother fled from island
My father fled from desert
and I am fleeing tendon and bone,
haunted and haunting
the only place I call home.

I stare at my own displacement
In disbelief,
In disgust.
Only the most wretched among us
would turn skin into tombstone
and their own hollow into grave.
I'm (dis)grace.

I wonder how my ancestors did it.
How they held the spirit and the semen
of the colonizer between their jagged teeth.
How they housed cruelty adjacent to wisdom.
Violence alongside intuition.
Did they feel volatile?

Did they erupt into magnificent disaster?
My body\\ prepares for your eviction.
The earth will always take back
what is rightfully hers.

Healing does not bother herself
with who's left in her wake
once she wakes.
Like how the ocean demands to exist entire,
without apology
without pause

She's got the tenacity
of weeds and of storms.
Her growth is not spiteful,
not toxic, nor sin.
It's the inevitable aftermath
of (dis)grace.

Taino Teeth

Taino Teeth
are shaped like shovels.
And so,
are mine.

Every bite I take, I dig
a grave for the lie:
that we no longer exist,
that we are not enough
of a people
to count
as being alive,
that there once
was a successful
genocide.

My incisors sharpen like spades:
they are hungry
to unearth
a world
where there is no longer
a need
to question who we are
and how we came to be.

Recovery

I'm not interested in recovery.
What would I recover?
The body I used to have?
The person I used to be?
Impossible.
Give me scar tissue.
Give me calcified bone.
Give me joints that ache with the weather.
Give me tougher.
Give me tender.
Give me body.
Give me soul.
And I will love them.
I will love them.

Introductory Thoughts // The (Dis)possession of the Body: On Genocide, Trauma, and Becoming Ghosts

When a traumatic event occurs, it can often be hard to contain it. Trauma has a tendency to ripple and to extend beyond itself. Like water, it leaks through every crevice it can find. Trauma clings to bodies, and yet it refuses to solely be contained within the body. Trauma makes it hard for me to discern where I end and where you begin. It makes it hard for me to discern where I begin and my ancestors end.

Humans are known to be incredibly empathic creatures. When we see others in pain, we feel something: pain, grief, anger, a desire to help. When a large-scale harm occurs, like the assassination of a president or an attack of war, a phrase we often hear is that a "nation has gone into mourning." In this sense, strangers mourn strangers because of a common national identity, but they will always be strangers. *Perhaps you can relate, then: that when my people hurt, I hurt.*

Grief is a connecting force. Grieving is a social and political act, and so too must be healing.

As Edward C. Valandra writes, "genocide is the trauma."[1] History has taught us that the United States was born out of colonial violence on black, indigenous, and mixed race bodies. Along with the earth, our bodies have bared the brunt of colonization through rape, incarceration, medical abuse, state sanctioned violence, war violence, alcoholism and addiction, epidemics of suicide, decreased life expectancy, high birth mortalities, and reactions to environmental racism. These manifestations are current and continual; they are not over. "Colonization is a structure, not an event."[2] Therefore, our bodies remember past harm while simultaneously enduring new harm. Our bodies are physical places where colonization and trauma become one and the same.

In psychology, trauma is most widely understood through a diagnosis of Post-Traumatic Stress Disorder (PTSD). One symptom of PTSD is

---

[1] Valandra, Edward. "Decolonizing 'Truth': Restoring More than Justice." *Justice as Healing: Indigenous Ways.* Ed. Wanda D. McCaslin. (2005).
[2] Wolfe, Patrick. "Settler colonialism and the elimination of the native." *Journal of Genocide Research.* (2006).

dissociation. Psychology understands dissociation as a symptom or set of symptoms that contributes to a person feeling unreal, or outside of themselves. Dissociation is a type of detachment, or a disconnected experience that occurs after a traumatic event. Dissociation can feel like being forced from our bodies. For people who are targeted by genocide, this forced leaving from our bodies can feel reminiscent of the forced leaving of our people from our lands.

As I write, I write from the specific position that I hold as a queer, trans, and mixed race person with Jewish, Taino, African, and Spanish ancestry. From this position, this writing has become deeply personal. My peoples have been dispossessed of our land, our cultures, our spiritualities, and our bodies for centuries or longer. My ancestors and living kin have learned to survive within conditions that have wanted us dead or dying, or at least out of the way. I spent much of my childhood trying to be as out of the way as possible, trying to leave to avoid being harmed. When I couldn't physically remove my body from racial violence, I started removing something else. I began excavating; I began evicting; I began dying. I often move through the world feeling like I am not in my body, that I am kept outside of it. Sometimes, I think I hold so much grief that my body doesn't have enough room in it for me.

I write with political intent. I am invested in the healing of peoples who have been targeted by genocide. There is a common experience among us that is worth understanding as academics, educators, and liberation-workers. There are so many lenses that we can use to expose that experience: trauma studies, critical theory, biopolitics, psychology, epigenetics, art. The experience has different names and frameworks: dissociation, post-traumatic stress, ancestral trauma. I personally call it a form of "becoming ghost."

In the queer of color communities that I have found myself in, I have noticed many people publicly naming themselves as ghosts through music, art, etc. It has become so commonplace to see the use of this metaphor that it catalyzed my exploration into this phenomenon. It might go without saying that ghosts are dead things. Thus, the imagery of a ghost is particularly jarring when applied to people who have been targets of genocide. Why is it that so many of us feel that we are already dead? Who and why are we haunting? And, who gets to feel fully alive?

Dissociation interrupts life. It occurs when bodies are under extreme stress or perceiving danger. When this happens, bodies go into "Fight," "Flight," or "Freeze" mode. Dissociation is most closely related to the freeze response. In freeze, the body gets stuck; it can't move, do, or be the way that it normally does. Many people will experience a fight, flight, or freeze response at some point in their lives, but often these responses are temporary. However, sometimes danger is all around us and we can't escape it. For peoples who are survivors of genocide, living in a world where colonization still prevails, there is no escaping harm. Thus, there is no escaping the physiological effects of being harmed. Bodies under stress all the time falter, fatigue, and fuck up. Bodies under stress all the time become unsafe and unreliable homes.

There is research in epigenetics on historical and intergenerational trauma and its impact on the body. In a study of the Dutch famine in the 1940s,[3] it was recorded that babies of mothers who had experienced starvation during their pregnancy were born with a low birth weight. This is not necessarily revelatory; it is to be expected because of a lack of nutrients during their gestation. However, when looking at the grandchildren of those women, scientists noticed that these babies were also born with low birth weights. This study suggests that trauma can affect our genetics in a way that is much more rapid than thousands of years of evolution. For African Americans, this passing-down-of-trauma has been researched by Joyce DeGruy in her renowned book, *Post-Traumatic Slave Syndrome*.[4] DeGruy argues that patterns, behaviors, beliefs, and feelings that were responses to being enslaved are still being carried by African Americans today. While her work is solely about the effects of slavery, the concepts can be applied more broadly to other manifestations of genocide and colonization. Understanding epigenetics and ancestral trauma can offer us insight to how hundreds of years of colonization might be impacting black, brown, and indigenous peoples today. While the academy is slowly but surely picking up questions regarding ancestral trauma, its conclusions are

[3] Carey, Nessa. *The Epigenetics Revolution: How Modern Biology Is Rewriting Our Understanding of Genetics, Disease, and Inheritance.* (2012).
[4] Degruy, Joy. *Post Traumatic Slave Syndrome: America's Legacy of Enduring Injury and Healing.* (2005).

merely offering colonial legitimacy to what many indigenous peoples have known for so long: that our bodies are deeply connected to our ancestors.

Feeling dead, as peoples who are targeted by genocide, may not be pure coincidence. We must come to terms with the fact that, if dissociation makes us feel like ghosts, then we are experiencing a kind of "deadness" that is perhaps related, if not caused by, the murders and forced relocation of our peoples. The metaphor of the ghost gives us language to understand the spiritual and psychological manifestations of genocide. I am arguing that dissociation is a symptom or product of genocide, that oppression and colonization can cause PTSD, and that all people have the right to feel fully alive in our bodies.

Ghosts are haunting. Looking to the western portrayal of ghosts in movies and media, the trope of the ghost is a character that has "unfinished business" left in the waking world. Ghosts are traumatized subjects, and perhaps this is why they feel so familiar. Like us, they are beings who have experienced great hurt, grief, loss, or violence. They have yet to receive closure, they are seeking (something, anything). Ghosts are the remnants of harmed humanity, the yearning for a different resolution. In spite of the harm, ghosts embody a unique kind of hopefulness; their hopefulness fuels their haunting until they find closure, peace, healing.

Sometimes, I am a ghost. I'm harmed, and haunting, and yearning for resolution. We are all created ghosts. Our bodies are haunted as they are haunting. We are simultaneously haunted by historical legacies of colonization[5] as we continue to haunt colonial spaces. Our bodies are possessed, leaving our spirits dispossessed. This dispossession functions as a support beam of racial and colonial capitalism. Colonization thrives when its targets disconnect from our bodies; we become more compliant, more easily exploitable, less resistant. When not in our bodies, we don't become revolutionaries, or visionaries, or healers. We assimilate. We collude. We lose touch with our own humanity, and the humanity of others.

Healing can never equate to assimilation.[6] Therefore, healing

---

[5] Tuck, Eve. *Glossary of Haunting*. (2013).
[6] McCaslin, Wanda D. "Introduction." *Justice as Healing: Indigenous Ways*. Ed. Wanda D. McCaslin. (2005).

cannot render us into a more "normal" way of feeling or being. It also cannot bring us back to before harm occurred. Instead, healing must be generative and creative; it must connect us to the ways of our peoples and move us away from embodying and adopting colonialism in any form. To heal with the ghost we must name it. We must confront it. We must give it a place to speak. To tell a story is to wield both weapon and medicine. To tell a story is to preserve cultural memory. But, dissociation has taken so many stories from us. We are taught to forget in order to assimilate. From a physiological standpoint, when trauma manifests as dissociation, it can be especially difficult to hold onto memory. Memory is sacred; it reminds us who we were, who we are, and who we can become. Between these conscious and unconscious forms of forgetting, we lose sense of ourselves, and with it, the ability to tell the stories that need to be told.

So instead, I'm here to tell you a ghost story.

Spell #3: On Grief

I invite my ancestors and the universe that have always held me to be present with me as I grieve, and to hold the following reminders close to me, so that I will not forget what is true, that:

1. Grieving is the hardest thing we will ever do.
2. Grief demands to be witnessed, so I will invite others to grieve with me and to hold me in my grief.
3. I will let the tears flow without judgment and without force. I will recognize this as my body's way of healing and of moving grief out of me. Grief must be felt, but it need not be held captive.
4. I will give myself permission to feel every feeling that comes, even the ugly ones. I will hold the wisdom that each feeling is both temporary and crucial.
5. Every loss is a catalyst for deep transformation within me. I must grieve whoever or whatever I lost, and I must simultaneously grieve the person I used to be before this loss.
6. Grief is not the enemy. Grief is the process. Grief is the healing. It is through grief that we find answers to our oldest questions, that we find resolution for our deepest wounds. I have the power to steer the ship of grief through every rough water. I get to decide what grief makes of me.

The Legend of the Coquí

Legend has it that the coquí cries for the mothers of lost children

Chrrrrp Chrrrrp

These tiny bodies
write the soundtrack
for the entire island.
Mothers' grief
is all our grief to hold.

And yet,
over time, the never-ending echo
fades out of focus, shifts into backdrop.
We tune out
what is familiar.
We imagine silence
where it has never been.

In America,
the pain of a people
paints the back walls
of the barrio
where my mother was born.

At every turn
racismo clicked in her ears
Chrrrrp Chrrrrp
The footsteps of cockroaches
Chrrrrp Chrrrrp
her hunger begging to be soothed
Chrrrp
the sirens
Chrrrp
the slurs
Chrrrp
the struggle
Chrrrp Chrrrrp Chrrrp

the Grief

worn in our ears
our whole lives—
like the song of the coquí.

Will you stop to pay respect
to the mothers who still
grieve all that they have lost?
To the mothers
inside us all?

Legend has it
that the homeland
still mourns those of us
who've been taken away.
Though we may not yet be dead,
we know death intimately—
we were raised in a country
built on it
and we let that death in.

I listen closely
and still feel the *chrrrp*-ing
conspicuous as a heart
beating a child to sleep
because

Legend has it
that through the coquí,
Puerto Rico still cries
for me.

Northampton, MA

This is a heartbreak town.
They've got the cemeteries
next to playgrounds.
They teach the children to grieve
before they teach them to love.

The crickets are louder than the thunder.
The cicadas are louder than the crickets.
I climbed to the top of the mountain
just to watch the hawks play.
They're the last ones who remember how.
Sadly, they too are migratory.
Temporary beings in a temporary place,
hungry for somewhere else.
They all know better than to stay
where the sun plays tricks,
where everything
is slightly more dangerous
than it seems.

This is a town
that makes ghosts out of people
and calls it justice.
A town that sucks marrow from your bone
and calls it a "small-town thing."
The puritans are still fucking in the cemeteries
because it's the only place
that won't judge them for their sins.
They think they are summoning
the next sexual revolution from beyond the grave.
The only spirit that comes
is the sweet smell of racial purity—
this is a town where white people fall in love with their whiteness.
They settle into it.
May their ancestors be proud.

This is a heartbreak town
for anyone who doesn't belong here.
Like me, and like you.

I'm sure you looked like a hawk in the middle of September
preparing to depart.
And I'm sure I looked like a small human
atop a mountain,
in awe.

I loved you in the in-between.
I loved you in this genocidal ghost town.
We were neither dying nor dead,
but still, we kept haunting.

I guess it's fitting then,
that you met me
on the border of the playground and the cemetery.
Like a child,
you taught me to grieve
before you ever taught me to love.

Lapse

My therapist said it might get worse before it gets better.
The healer said that when you experience loss,
your body remembers every loss you've ever had.

No one prepared me for how gravity would feel like weightlessness.
How standing would feel like falling out of a plane.
How love would feel like the dull edge of a blade.
No one ever said that nightmares would feel easier than getting out of
bed.
I am mourning myself even though I don't want to.
I'm trying not to vomit from the smell of this rotting carcass inside me.
I used to say that connection is more powerful than our trauma.
I used to say that everything is temporary, even this body.
I used to say that I live to rebirth myself over and over again.

I am trying to remember.
But I don't know how.

The Home She Made Me

I will love her
like pent up sunlight
like pent up rage
like raw sugar refusing process
like roots refusing soil
reusing the names they gave us
burying shame like we don't need it anymore

I know that we were both trying
and I know that we were both still
we were still and we were trying
we were still trying to love each other better than before

I know that.

I told her once that our bodies
were the blueprints
to the kind of love neither of us
ever knew we needed

And with that,
I gave her permission to become the contractor.

it takes a certain kind of someone
to witness the beauty of someone else bursting
and to not notice, too, the devastation of it

to intentionally take scalpel to skin
to dig beneath organs
and find the vulnerability hiding underneath

to reach inside, pull it out
and leave herself there in its place

she made a mess of my insides
tied my intestines to her trauma
burrowed into my marrow
turned me into shelter
where she could store all the hurt
she never learned to hold herself

I promised to love it for her
to nurture the most fucked up parts of her
to remind her how necessary to this world
someone like her must be

even as she shoved her fingers down my throat
stained my walls with a mix of alcohol, salt, and negligence
she Destroyed my body
the only place I ever called home

the thing they don't tell you
is that queer people of color
Rape each other too

they don't tell you
that this betrayal
will hurt more than any other wound
in your legacy

I want us both
to never again
confuse abuse with love
codependence with friendship
this mess that was our relationship with
the most revolutionary thing we could possibly do

the truth is, I want her
to be able to do laundry at my house
without having to pretend that the panic
doesn't come in like a hurricane
that the post-traumatic stress
doesn't make my floorboards buckle
or my rafters shake
I want her
to put down roots
in this small town
without feeling displaced
without telling myself
that if she finds belonging here
I must belong elsewhere

some days,
I want to rake her name through the mud
ruthlessly call out the violence
drown in the vengeance
fill this whole valley with the sound of my grief
stagnate in the sound of it echoing back to me

but instead, I hold it where she used to sleep
somewhere between my gut and my ribs
somewhere between the knowledge that ruining her life
won't give me back mine
and the conviction that her liberation
is part of why I still fight

after the storm
I know that forgiveness will drip from the rooftops
I'll stare out my window, watching it
and remember that there's so much more for me
beyond this safe little home that I live in

and I will remember, too
that there is so much more out there for her
beyond the safe little home she built inside me

Grad School Lessons

How to fall asleep alone
How to grieve
How to write 30 pages on something that could be said in a sentence
How to let love in from unexpected places
How to be in pain
How to be alone but not lonely
How to tap out
How to forgive myself
How to grieve
How to stretch time
How to lose
How to let it go
How to be coerced
How to recognize coercion
How to become codependent with strangers (then how to not do that)
How to share space with someone who has been abusive to me
How to protect myself
How to set boundaries
How to grieve
How to stop trying to save people
How to stop avoiding doctors
How to save myself
How to run
How to cook
How to breathe
How to shovel a driveway full of snow
How to stop smiling at strangers
How to forget what home feels like
How to grieve
How to get back up
How to build myself humbler
How to hold myself steadier
How to live without the ocean
How to cut myself some slack
How to be present
How to be here
How to be healing
How to be whole

ANM // What will we do with this grief?

1.

You know, I always say that another world can't come unless we're
ready to let this one go.
But I wasn't ready to let you go.
I wasn't ready to give you back to the stars and the earth and the wind
and the fire.
I didn't learn enough from you.
I'm filled with so much gentleness,
that I'll never get to give to you.
Please, tell me what to do with it.

The birds woke me up this morning
with a love song for the departed.
The dragonflies keep visiting
to bear witness to the grief you left behind.

We could bury it in the ground.
Ask gravity and soil to keep it down in the trenches
so far from our bodies.
We could measure our healing in minutes and days,
but for whom?

There's no good way to grieve
There's no good way to breathe
There's no good way to heal

But we do it
Every day
We do

2.

The scientists say nothing is created nor destroyed,
even if it feels that way.
Nothing is created,
and nothing is destroyed.

If you look carefully,
you'll see there's not really a reason for everything,
but it's reasonable to believe that there could be.

I'm not there yet.
I'm not holding the universe on my palm.
I'm not looking for anything that matters.
There's not enough matter in this world

to make up the loss of spirit,
of gift,
or of hope.

If nothing is destroyed
then, where did you go?

Hope is the thing we lose most easy
through the holes in the pockets of our chests.
I swallow it sometimes.
Like medicine.
Like tonic.
Like tongue.

Why is it that the people who teach hope the best
are often the ones who feel it the worst?

3.

You were killed by no one's fault,
but inheritance
of all the trauma and grief of generations reproducing in our bodies and
our lands and our peoples.

It's too much to ask one human to heal it all away,
and yet we do it
Every day
We do

I know you wanted to heal just as bad as the rest of us.
I'm so sorry you weren't given the chance.
I'm sorry for this world for which we are all responsible.

We will commit to building something better.
We will remember your brilliance and your pain.
We will hold it in our mouths when we speak,
and our feet as we make the path by walking.

Nothing is created nor destroyed,
but we'll create it, anyway.

The scientists say every action has an equal and opposite reaction.
So, let our reaction be to live fully, to love well, to remember that grief
and joy move through the same parts of our bodies,

to be gentle, to be tender, to be here.

Spell #4: On Loving Our People

I invite my ancestors and the universe that have always held me to create space for the most revolutionary love there is.

1. There is no scarcity in love, only abundance.
2. Love is not fragile, it is the fiercest thing we do.
3. We practice what liberation feels like when we allow ourselves to be vulnerable, tender, and sweet with the ones we love.
4. This sweetness, in the context of a world full of struggle and oppression, is the seedling for our freedom. The more we nurture it, the more space it takes up. The more space it takes up, the more power we have to overshadow the violence and trauma.
5. We cannot forget that we are interdependent beings, that to be human is to love, that the soul yearns for intimacy with others.
6. Love requires accountability and a deep commitment to the self. It requires a willingness to change, to heal, and to become the kind of people who create the world we want to live in, together.

I love you.
I love you.
I love you.

Say it three times to remind ourselves
that we were never the problem.
That this,
right here,
is the one thing that never needs to be unlearned.

I Would Tell You that I Know

If only you would whisper into my ear
something like:
I feel the sadness expanding through each inflated lung;
it's caught up in my inhalation and every
breath I take fills my chest
with gravity, it would feel better
to let myself fall into slumber.

I would tell you that I know. And, you can be sad tonight.
I will hold you here.

If only you would scream into my ear
something like:
I feel the anger shattering my veins
each time my heart sends a booming plea
through to the tips of my fingers
and they can't help but shake
with every explosion, it would feel better
to let my fists beat into this broken glass.

I would tell you that I know. And, you can be angry tonight.
I won't be scared of you here.

If only you would mutter into my ear
something like:
I feel inside myself, my thoughts are too loud
and my lips too still;
the voices around me are static
and I don't care to decipher
these tangled tones right now, it would feel better
to just be left alone.

I would tell you that I know. And, you can be alone tonight.
I will leave you here; I promise I won't go far.

But there are nights where all you can tell me is:
I feel empty.

And I weep into your neck, wishing you would feel
anything else.

The Lesson

Here is a terrible resolve:
Unspeak.
Here is the way to return:
Unlove.

I am writing my worst fears into my bedroom wall.
I am counting the fingerprints I've left on my bathroom sink.
I can't clean up the mess I've been living.

Wistful fervor. Take me back to where the heron crows.
Take me back to where the marsh fills up the in-between.
Where the sky pays a penance to the wishful youth.

We resist not one tremor, but all of the ways that we quake like the
earth—uncontrollably.

I'm living the same way I did when I was 10.
I'm living the same way I did when I was 16.
I am not a record. Don't spin me right round.
Don't make me vomit in your mouth.

I am living like a tarantula. I am living like a black widow.
I am a spider in a child's body. I am a child in a woman's body.
Get me out of here, alive.

Stern looks stir up all the old ways of feeling.
I feel small. I feel like I am falling off a cliff.
My fingers only know how to slip.
You can put a stake through my palm
or you can let gravity take me.
Either way, I might wish for death
and you will wish that I stop saying that.

Can you hear the open wounds asking me to bleed? Can you hear the
trauma asking me to bleed?
I can't tell which screams louder.

I blanket the whole town with the sound of my grief.
I cushion my heart from any chance of abandon.
You are not the way out, so let me find a new one.
The lesson in this mess is not that I have finally figured out how to grow

up.
It's that I'm still spinning webs around myself.
It's that my body is a ghost I will never know.
It's that this method of survival is painful,
but loving you
was more so.

Burn

I've got blood like pine sap
Sweet & Thick
I'm sticking to your Tongue & your Teeth
I'm like tar against your sullied palms
Pray to me like you Pray to these woods.
Tell me you want more of me in your mouth.
Tell me you want more of me.
and I'll say, "baby you know I would
but tonight I'm like these maple trees.
tonight, you've got me all tapped out."

I've got a love like a forest fire.
I'm waiting for the ash in my chest
to turn cancerous.
I'm waiting to be devoured.
leaf to finger to root
Charred skin, Soil blacked.

I'll taste better than you ever did
outside on a hazy day
it's getting harder to breathe
I'll fuck better than you ever did
you can come like a smoke-cloud
and I'll be the easiest thing to leave

Falling

Once, I fell without looking.
Caught up scrying,
I forgot to check
where I stepped, missed the mess
that the future set on my door.
Where's the warning?
Is there a better way
to hit the ground running
than to fall without looking?

I fell into the arms of a mason.
He carved stories out of stone.
He carved my face out of marble.
He built cities from ruins
and ruined the place that we stood for so long.
I was young and he was aging into greed.
I was love and he was hating to feel
what was under the bitter need
of needing only what was wanted,
the filthy desire of giving nothing
but a promise to give in.
I was hope but he was hoping for more.

I gave up drinking
when I found the sun
at the bottom
of the bottle.
Smash shame
into the ground.
There are seashells
in the desert town that he left me.
There is sound in the quiet that he left me.
If you go under,
I'll go up.
Tell me where I'm going.
I'm going to fill myself up.
Go to the rum shed.
Go to the thunder.
Get out of heavy.
Fight heartfelt through song.
Sob.

Get out of your head.
Get out of his.
We've all got to know how it feels
to fall head first.
Histamine and sting.
Sink down into the thick
of the growth you've steered clear of.
The carnivores are waiting on the outside.
They'll push you in and make you bleed.
Rethink tenacity.
Rethink your next birth.
Do you know where you're going,
or will you bleed yourself dry?

I used to remember these words
that I'm writing. I used to remember
the words that I wrote. I
used to remember the name of my
love. I used
to remember the way
I would run into the woods.
As if the woods would catch me
when I fell.
As if by falling,
I would be better
than I was.

I would be dirty.
I would be bruised.
I would be broken.
I would be wounded.
I would be cut up.
I would be split open.
I would be holding the earth in my body.
I would be closer to holding myself by the roots.
I would be closer to holding myself up for once.

SM//Trigger

You wanted Orion's Belt
etched into your back
in permanent, black, ink.

There is a black belt
tied around my neck
and you knew exactly how hard to pull.

Make me remember
Shatter.

Make me remember
all the ways I do not matter.

You ruined the night sky.
You ruined counting constellations.

You will not be the one to ruin me.

A New Kind of Ruin

My dreams try to tell me that enough has not been made of me. I can feel a thousand wings caught in this incessant cage of a body; every way out has been locked down.

I can feel like flutter. I can feel like beat-against-the-door. I can feel like the walls can't cave in fast enough. I want to be covered in a new kind of ruin.

I'm worried about the forecast. I'm worried about the way the sun can't touch the bottom of the sea. There are memories there. There are bodies there, aching for revival. I am just another.

Watch me get lost inside the mirror. A lovely image of you and I, deception and desire. The Death Card can't come quick enough. There are a thousand wings to find and I know you toy with trying them all on. Can we will the spirits to act in our favor? Can we will the spirits to grant us this amnesty?

Caress the instinct of it all. Bless your intuition. I'll be won over with brilliance, like the shadows cast. Like the wisdom buried deep underground. You can't teach me how to breathe, but you can do it with me.

Caution, like bone growth, is a heavy weight to carry. It will slow us down, but how else are we to practice strength? How else are we to lift ourselves out of becoming another untold story, sinking in the sea?

The human in us is not too old to break up with our habits. We can untwine our cells from memory. We can unresolve conviction. Let me abandon the sweet seduction of follow. Detach me from the currents that have carried me to you, and away.

I know now about the exit. Fate sat me down and told me how it has to be—

You can't teach me how to love, dear. But you can do it with me.

Healing

Healing is still—
is always—
possible.

when we heal
ourselves—
together—
our ancestors
heal
with us.

GGN //Before I Met Them

I.
Before I met them
Gray was the color of the sky for eight months of the year
when my body forgets what to call itself
and I put grace and health
into my bones, stored alongside 2000 IUs
of synthesized sun
Gray was the color
of waiting for the aching
to hit me like the rain
of warning signs and taking every hour like a battle in a war
Gray was the color of everything I needed to escape:
this winter
this small city
this pacific northwest grim
these passive aggressive ways of saying
I want to belong here,
but I don't

II.
When you meet them
they'll put their name into your mouth
like a promise to themself
that they'll never be confused
for someone else
they've got secrets written in the stars
and their palms are heavy from the constellations
they held on their heart line
they carved them down into art for the walls they've been building
they've been building since they lost their first love.
they've been building a way out of needing to stay
since the land beneath their feet felt untrusting
of every wrong move they made
they made stillness out of running away

and if you're lucky you'll be running alongside them
finding solace in the edges of things
if you're lucky they will teach you about bodies
about being whole
and being perfect
and being ugly in the beings we've been building

and if you're lucky they will love you
and the clouds would give way
and in clearing, we'd hear the universe say:
"This…this is what the darkness was for"

III.
Once, we were leaving the space where our lovers left us
we were the type to keep giving into the void
we planted in the fallow
burned the final embers
we were relentless
we were loyal
we let ourselves fall without letting go
until they said:
no more of this
I am worthy of growing my own love
I am worthy of growing myself home

IV.
Gray is the way I came back
to loving the way I want to be loved

in our bodies there is art
we built this in our bodies
in our bodies we belong

To all the Jewish people of color who feel caught between the various debates about anti-racism vs anti semitism

We do not have to pick sides. We do not have to wait for Solomon's judgement before being torn apart. Racism and anti-semitism are both real. Both are painful, both are ours to grieve and to fight. We can be angry about racism in Ashkenazi and White Jewish spaces, be angry about the genocide that Israel commits in the name of our people, and simultaneously be angry about anti-semitism in communities of color and anti-racist spaces. We know that racism and anti-semitism are not always two distinct systems or ideologies. That our bodies serve as the intersection where they become one. That from our vantage point, it's always both. That while we are often overlooked and forgotten, we are also neither isolated nor alone. We get to be deeply connected to all other JPOC, people of color, and Jewish people.

So, in case you (like me) have yet to hear it, I see you, I'm thinking of you, and I'm with you.

Self-Love

I don't have time to wait for you
to learn how to love me
with the kind of gentleness
I offer myself each day.

It's taken me lifetimes
to learn how to
hold my belly and
kiss my shoulders
without asking God for a body
that could bend without breaking.
I've spent too long believing
I would never be whole.

I owe myself
this much:
a love that is
all mine.

Spell #5: On Coming Home

I invite my ancestors and the universe who have always held me to support me in holding myself accountable to the following intentions, to bring me home:

1. To trust myself, my gut, my mind, my intuition, my body, and my instinct
2. To develop my strength physically and emotionally
3. To be aware of my boundaries and enforce them
4. To access deep and high wisdom, to draw upon ancestral knowledge, to believe in my own intellect and capacities
5. To move through the world like I belong in it and with it
6. To nourish myself and my soul
7. To write and create more
8. To recharge, re-energize, rejuvenate, rejoice, recollect, regenerate (to allow goodness, kindness, and compassion to flow through me again)
9. To trust that the universe is holding me, that the right energy will rise where it needs to, that there will be enough time, that I, alone, do not have the capacity to ruin anything
10. To find grounding and centering with ease, to maintain clarity and connection
11. To exist in and with my own body
12. To decorate myself only in ways that bring me joy
13. To commit to my own spiritual practices, and deepening my spiritual commitment and craft
14. To remember that I do not exist in isolation, but that I belong with so many

A Partial Life Story

1. An Atlantic island birthed me, much (un)like my mother's.
2. A bridge connects the city to my home. I am a bridge, too.
3. Brown child, white child. Depends who you ask. Did you ever ask her?
4. The east coast gave me to the malice of the clean white west. I learned what it meant to be derelict.
5. I turned into stone. I devoured myself whole.
6. Migration is one of those things that never leaves your body.
7. I preferred the company of people far away from here. They never knew their luck to practice the act of staying.
8. Too young to vote, but not to learn. Baby, what are you doing in a place like this?
9. Once, I had a love like oleander. Toxic from root to tip. I gave up trying to nurture out the poison.
10. Maybe there's something to be said of the teeth of men.
11. Storytelling: the art of speaking while remembering. If you ask me to try, I will tell you: I forget how it goes, I forget how it goes. Until one day, I really do.
12. Death came with seizures. Seizures came with drugs. Drugs came with sadness. Sadness came from all things at once. Death came from living. Living came from death.
13. Doctors and teachers are both hoods in disguise.
14. I never tried not to be a statistic. It's not our fault the odds are stacked against us.
15. I outsourced intimacy. There could be no ties to the place I rest my head.
16. Once, I had a love like dandelions who showed me we are not ruining the land by existing. We don't need to be flowers to know that we belong.
17. I put my soul into knowing and unlearning the lie.
18. They'd name mountains after us if only they, too, knew the truth.
19. Families are built out of struggle. Mine has been built many times over.
20. I've been walking and walking and waiting.

For now, I dig my toes in and stay.

Healer, Rise Up

There are only so many things we can take into the grave,
but this trauma will not be one of them.
There are only so many memories we get to carry in a lifetime,
what would I remember
if this genocide
hadn't made a home out of my bones?

I don't know how many oceans I've been asked to carry for my
ancestors. how many witnesses have watched me drown in them. Must I
have the hugeness of continents,
the muscle of mountains
to contain it?

As a child, I had to be bigger than an island
more rigid than the sand
just to hold it all in place
just to keep it from spilling. Everywhere.

My
lungs collapse while diaspora crashes like tidal waves.
Gasping for air while dysphoria builds settlements inside the wound.

My motherland is my mother's land,
there is nothing for me there.
(My tongue touches all the wrong places in my mouth and I might
as well spit up blood before I spit out my first name, a name I cannot
pronounce.)

hurricane spears say, this island isn't safe for you.
uranium knives say, this water isn't safe for you.
debt daggers say, unsafety will always follow you.

I have become a servant for a place I no longer belong.

My ancestors ask too much of me.
They don't understand all that I cannot do.
I don't have enough boy in me to soldier up.
I don't have enough boy in me to leave behind the girl in me.
She wants someone to hold her at night.
She insists that I'm the only man for the job.

But I've been married off to America.
I've been married off to mixed blood and confused gender.
I've been married off to the storm inside my chest.
I am married to the wounds of my ancestors.
They have nestled inside my body like it is the last safe place we have left.
Because it is.
But

there is only so much that we can take into the grave.
There are only so many memories we can bury inside our bones.
I'm starting to think there's not enough room in me
for me.

I refuse to let this be my purpose,
to become another vessel
for the aches of generations to lay siege.
Instead,
tell the soldier to stand down
and the healer to rise up.

Breathe In.

Tell my mothers that I will love them, but I cannot carry them.
Tell my ancestors that I cannot hold them, but I will not leave them.
Tell the island that I forgive her, and the mainland that I don't (that I never will).
Tell myself that boundaries are medicine,
that "no" is not lonely.

Breathe Out. Let go.
Let go.

Remembering the from

A thousand years
                    descend and

raise
         the child
                    in a sphere of joy.

What do you think?
                    Will you allow

                                                  this shift?

swim. // sibling.

swim.
swim because
we were born
from islands.
we were born
in warm waters
we were born
into a history
of wombs
giving birth
to warriors.
swim because
they told us
we would die
before
we found
the shore.

well,
we shored
up, alright.
we shored up
on a place
that don't feel
like home.
because it's not.

this land
is not ours,
just like Vieques
never belonged
to the navy,
does not belong,
to the hotel
seducing temporary settlers
via gay cruises
and spring vacations.

do not forget
that we
are vacationing
here.
swim not because
there is
a home
in Vieques
waiting for us.
it's not ours,
either.

swim
because we are
the ones waiting.
we spent our
whole lives waiting
for each other
to learn to
master the sea
well enough
to keep
the other
from drowning.

we're learning now
how important
it is
not to drift
without making waves.

keep making waves.
the ocean will
forgive, the ocean
is many things.

first, god
but also
predator and
also asylum.

don't get comfortable
in silence.

keep kicking
your feet
because one day
the ocean
will grant us
the gift
and we won't
have to swim
anymore.

Diaspora

we are a broken people
who found Home
in an Ocean
called Grief

the thing about that is
you can't find Stillness
in an Ocean

the waves knock you down
before your feet can remember
the way the flat earth
whispers Steady
the way the soil mimics Womb

sometimes the salt feels too thin
to offer Holding
sometimes the water feels too thick
not to drown
sometimes my Body feels too alone in this wake
even when you are just a stone's throw
Beneath

we used to wish to beach like Whales
to learn to walk
on the backwashed shore
to become a mirror of our oldest Ancestors—
the ones who left the Goo that made us
so they could learn fire, shelter, Order.
we used to wish to find a place
to call our own
to become a People
of some kind
again

I think a better wish
might be for cleaner waters
and gills

Father-Trauma

He doesn't cry, but he almost does—
I see it in the way he holds his fingers
to his palms.
He's holding it all in
like there's something more than sadness
to keep hidden from his daughter
like there's a person
in her father
that he won't let her see.
She sees distance.
She sees pride.
She sees distance.
He can try to paddle forward,
but the tide only carries those
who choose to float.
Throw the heaviness
to the undertow.

Won't you meet me
where the horizons
all look the same
and where crying
to the sea
isn't quite as scary
as being out here
all alone.

A Poem from the Bottom of the Ocean

i never could take a hit
never learned how to fall with grace
i've been wasting time
growing new bones to breakdown into dust
grind my honor into the fuel it takes to win this fight
i've been running on empty
driving myself into the ground
dignity don't come easy
for those of us who've been pummeled by the forces of gravity
and being born into existence
just to find out that we can't exist here

being isn't easy—
there is no manual to teach us how to fight for this shit
we're learning how to walk underwater
before anyone's ever thought up a way to learn how to swim
and i'm just wondering what it might feel like
to kick the weight away
and float for the first time

there must be something so simple
in all the things we don't yet know how to do
if we could see the whole damn picture
we'd know how much we're losing
by confusing these walls with safety
and by digging wells to relieve the aching of our bones

we get tired by midnight
curled up-side down and heartsick
because something isn't quite right
and you just don't know what it is
so you tell yourself
that something must be not quite right with you
and you succumb to the whitest of tongues that says

"Don't dare dream of anything more than the bottom of the ocean.
Don't dare ask for a way to touch sky.
Don't dare stand in protest.
Don't mention the people who have drowned here.
You've got worlds inside your body—
You better learn to keep them there."

this is a poem for the misunderstood
for the misguided
for the misfitted, heart-headed youth
who get told over and over again
that things will get better but it only gets better for a few
this is a poem for the teachers
who get so caught up teaching
that they never learn to unlearn
all the things they've been taught.
this is a poem for my mothers who won't understand it
and my mothers who write poetry in secret
this is a poem for the fist fights
for the black eyes, for the bruised ribs
for the nights we never left
because boys don't hurt girls like that
unless they really really like them
this is for the failed suicides—
the wounds left unattended
the ways we escaped the racist
sexist heterosexist ableist idea
that we're not good enough
and we never will be
this is for my younger self
who thought there weren't any answers
and this is for fighting off the feeling that we're in this all alone

we're not alone

we've just forgotten how to fight for anything more than the bottom
of the ocean
we've given into performing complacency, and patience, and good
behavior
we're driving ourselves into the ground

and there is something so very troubling
about the way a revolution
gets stopped before it starts.
so tell me—
how many times must the stones
be thrust upon our flesh
before we pick one up
and throw it back
we're out of ideas

descendant

out of breath
out of options
out of time if we ever had any
and the only thing we have left is a dream
lodged inside a body,
a question
lodged inside an answer,
anger and love
lodged inside cycles of violence

i'm not ready to let go of wanting more
i want more than just surviving
in a world that keeps on asking me to die

what's stopping us from pulling up the roots
to heal us from the inside out
must it hurt so much to uncover?
there may be another answer,
there will be another struggle,
after this one, after the last one
(we're in that one now)
we can't recover the bodies
but we can bury the mistakes

where there is sun, there is something left to do
turn light into (re)creation
god won't be mad if we take back the tools
and recycle
and remember

you will never learn to swim
if you are anchored to the ocean floor

Home

Last week, I picked up a divinity rod.
She pointed straight into the ocean
and said "walk this way home."

Sometimes, there are paths that we will never take
Simply because we believe we cannot.

My grandmother
practiced Santería in the concrete of New York,
but I'm not supposed to tell you that.
My mother
always told me not to play with magic.
"Don't trust in magic."
"Don't trust in blood."

When I was twenty
I had a friend tell me the same thing.
He was raised by catholic priests trained in the art of exorcism.
He believed I was under a spiritual attack
after finding a tarot deck in the front pocket of my backpack.

He told me that should I open the door to the spirits around me,
it would be impossible to close it.
That if you take a sledgehammer to a dam
it might be easy to bring it down,
but you can never put it back with all that water gushing.
"You cannot rebuild what you destroyed
when all you have
is a fucking sledgehammer."

Sometimes, we cannot keep out the things that we have let in.

But deep down I know
my family has been knocking down damns for centuries.
We've been abandoning religion for years.
We've been letting ghosts love us
for no other reason than they are the only ones who could.

And, I don't know if I believe in Santería.
I don't know if I believe in la virgen, el padre, el espíritu santo

descendant

I don't know if I believe in the spirits that we've named in creole
tongues,
in the religions we've built in secret
to preserve some semblance of the way we used to believe.

In diaspora, we are supposed to lose all sense of who we are.
So what is there left for me to find?
What is it that I feel?
Where do I go from here?

I wonder what mi abuela would say
about talking to spirits
about letting them in
about feeling close to something we cannot see.

On days I am unsure,
I pick up the divinity rod.
I listen to her whisper
"this way, home"
I feel my ancestors all around me
more and more each day
and if nothing else,

I believe
in the power
of that.

Matters of Joy

Now's not the time
to be proper
and prosperous
or wise.

It's the time to be deviant
defiant
and young.

This is the day
when we stand on our chairs
take off our shirts
and let our skin heal from the weariness of wallowing.

I'm tired of waiting.

So, let's throw all this business casual
along with its neoliberal bullshit
out the window.

This is the day when our great-great-grandmothers
will rumble in their graves
and remember a time when they were just like us.

Their offspring will stop chastising the rebels
and join in the revolution.
Machetes in hand,
come hand in hand with me.
Because forever isn't as long as we planned.

I propose we go to every TGI Fridays in town
take 5 balloons each
stand in a line and let them go one by one.

Taken from us, like everything else has been taken.

Only today we don't cry.
Let the ocean hold our tears.

Today we'll laugh
and pretend that the media looks like us
that the president sounds like us
and that we only have to be as old
as the skin we've grown into
because today is the day for pretending.

Dress up,
go ahead,
raid your mommy's closet
'cause we're going out tonight, boys.

Find your gender
at the bottom of your feet
we'll be running barefoot through the street
watching fireworks that were never really there
just wait for these gunpowder stars
to fall into your palms,

just wait.

They're the only light that ever really mattered
and even they can't keep themselves from burning out.
Just wait.

If we're not careful, we're going to burn out, too.

That's why sometimes
I want to pretend that nothing matters.
I want to leave it all behind.
I want to take a breath
and believe for a moment
that we've been breathing like this for years.
Let us breathe.
Let us be carefree.
The elite don't get to own that feeling.
They own too much of us already.

I want to pretend that nothing matters.
Because nothing matters
except for the pitter-patter of dancing feet

ghosting up from the empty road that looks back at us
where we used to cross
without looking both ways.
We trusted the land
so we could take over the street.
Have we forgotten that we used to dance
while we demanded retribution?

Carmen Leah Ascencio asks us to be accountable to our joy.
I want to know what that kind of love feels like
I want to feel it in my core
I want to hold it in my blood
I want to honor my fight
I want to honor my uppercut
I want to honor this Brooklyn and this Boricua
that have nestled themselves under my tongue
I want to forgive this body
for all the harm it's done.

I want to shout into the heavens.
I want to call upon my gods:
Tell me how to be joyous
in a world that has tried to teach me nothing but pain.

They whisper back:
it's a caged bird
that will first teach you how to sing.

and you will still receive postcards
from the years you spent losing sleep
but now child,
write yourself letters in your dreams.

leave them in the sidewalk cracks
in the dandelion patches
in the sand broken down from boulders.

we are like the weeds.
we are like erosion.
it is in our nature to be simultaneously
beautiful and forceful.

because nothing will ever matter
if we are not magnificently present
making everyone know how ferociously we can exist.

descendant's duty

"

descend and
descend,
descendant.

descend and
dissent and
ascend.
"

ABOUT THE AUTHOR

Romeo Romero is a Puerto Rican & Jewish bicoastal poet/educator who writes about diaspora, dysphoria, ancestors, and being a being in a body. They love playing in the ocean, climbing trees, and pretending to be both those things. Their day job is working with a youth-led restorative justice program, which gives them hope every day that the world we want is not only possible, but inevitable.

Made in the USA
Middletown, DE
24 June 2018